YEAR 3

COMPREHENSION AND VOCABULARY

Victoria Hazell

Illustrated by
Janice Bowles

Back to Basics Comprehension and Vocabulary Year 3

Reprinted 2015, 2016, 2018

ISBN: 978 1 74215 917 1

Published by Pascal Press
PO Box 250
Glebe NSW 2037
www.pascalpress.com.au
contact@pascalpress.com.au

Author: Victoria Hazell
Publisher: Lynn Dickinson
Editors: Shelley Barons and Kerry Davies AE
Design and illustration: Janice Bowles
Front Cover design: Deb Snibson, MAPG
Printed by Thumbprints

Acknowledgements
The author is grateful to Blake Education for kindly granting permission to reproduce extracts and illustrations from the following books:

Page 10, Linda Stocks, *Spider Soup*, illustrated by Steven Hallam, Gigglers, 2004.

Page 12, Lisa Thompson, *Forgetful Friday*, illustrated by Cliff Watt, Gigglers, 2011.

Page 16, Bren MacDibble, *Take Me to Your Leader*, illustrated by Nathan Jurevicius, Gigglers, 2002.

Page 18, Susan Knight, *Thing in the Fridge*, illustrated by Luke Jurevicius & Jason Pamment, Gigglers, 2010.

Page 22, Lisa Thompson, *Facing Fears*, illustrated by Cliff Watt, Gigglers, 2011.

Page 26, Susan Mansfield, *Polar Explorers*, Go Facts, 2008.

Page 30, Nicolas Brasch & Mark Stafford, *Technological Wonders*, Go Facts, 2009.

Page 32, Mark Stafford, *Body Systems*, Go Facts, 2007.

Page 36, Maureen O'Keefe, *Our Future in Space*, Go Facts, 2006.

Page 38, Nicolas Brasch, *Gold*, Go Facts, 2009.

Contents & Checklist

ABOUT THIS BOOK

This book is designed to review essential Comprehension and Vocabulary skills required in Year 3. It provides detailed explanations of how to comprehend fiction and non-fiction texts in a literal, interpretive and applied manner. Each comprehension unit features a text extract with questions requiring literal, interpretive and applied comprehension of the text.

Literal comprehension:
What did the author tell you? Refer directly to the text to find the answers.

Interpretive comprehension:
What did the author intend you to understand? Read back over the text and think about what you can conclude from the facts you are given.

Applied comprehension:
*What do **you** think?* Relate what you have read to real-life situations and your existing knowledge of the world.

Parents or carers are encouraged to read the full explanations, on pages 8–9 for fiction and pages 24–25 for non-fiction, with their children before they do the practice units, and to discuss the glossary words under each text extract.

If further instruction is required, provide this book to the class teacher for review. A plan can then be devised between parent or carer and the school to ensure that all basic concepts are fully understood and consolidated.

Helpful features

- ★ **10 Top tips** are provided in full on pages 6 and 7 and are featured on the Practise pages. Read the tips carefully before reading them with your child, explaining any difficult words to ensure that each concept is fully understood.
- ★ **5 Vocabulary units** (Units 3, 7, 11, 15 and 19) feature activities using the 100 high-frequency words relevant to Year 3 students.
- ★ **5 Quick quizzes** (Units 4, 8, 12, 16 and 20) feature words used in the preceding stories and reinforce understanding of specific vocabulary found in the texts.
- ★ **100 High-frequency words** are provided in the centre of the book to be removed, laminated and cut out to make flash cards for extra practice (see page 5).
- ★ **3 Tests** on pages 42–44, two comprehension tests and a high-frequency words test, are to be done on completion of all 20 units. These tests will check that the skills have been consolidated.
- ★ **BOB time! Back Of the Book.** At the end of most exercises, BOB will remind children to check the Answer section on pages 45–47 to make sure they are on the right track.

Ideas for using the Game Cards

The flash cards in the centre of the book feature 100 high-frequency words that Year 3 children should be able to recognise, read and spell.

Two players

Player 1 flashes a card and Player 2 reads each word and spells it out accurately (without looking at the card).

Player 1 looks at a card and reads each word aloud (one at a time). Player 2 repeats the word and then writes it down. If a word is incorrectly spelled, take time to practise and then ask to be tested once more.

One player

1. Place all the same colour cards face down in a pile. Turn them over one at a time and read the words on the card.

2. Put the card face down on a second pile and quickly write down the words before you forget them.

3. Check that you have spelled them correctly and move on to the next card.

4. Score yourself and try to improve each time. Practise the misspelled words by writing them each five times.

Place all cards face up.
Sort into two piles:
Pile 1: Words I know
Pile 2: Words I am learning
Read aloud each word in Pile 2 and add it to Pile 1 when you know all the words on the card.

Australian Curriculum Year 3

Recognise high-frequency sight words (ACELA1486)
Draw connections between personal experiences and the worlds of texts, and share responses with others (ACELT1596)
Read an increasing range of different types of texts by combining contextual, semantic, grammatical and phonic knowledge, using text processing strategies, for example monitoring, predicting, confirming, rereading, reading on and self-correcting (ACELY1679)
Use comprehension strategies to build literal and inferred meaning and begin to evaluate texts by drawing on a growing knowledge of context, text structures and language features (ACELY1680)

10 TOP TIPS

Helpful tips to gain full comprehension of a text

1

Main Idea

When we read, we can use features in the text to determine the main idea of the text. Looking for headings, bold print, pictures, captions and diagrams can help us work out what the text is mostly about.

So, look at the text and then ask:

"What is the main idea?"

2

Predictions

When we read, we think about what might happen next and make predictions based on what we know and what we have read so that we can find out the sequence of events.

So, read the text and then ask:

"What happens next?"

Cause and Effect

When we read, we can think about what caused something to happen and what the effect was. If you read a story or a newspaper article, it will always tell you what has happened and what caused it to happen.

So, read the text and then ask:

"What happened?" and

"What caused it to happen?"

Connections

When we read, we make connections between what we know, other things we have read and the text we are reading.

So, read the text and then ask:

"Does this remind me of something?"

"Is this situation like something that has happened to me?"

5

Inferences

When we read, we form our own ideas, or make inferences, about what we are reading. We can use clues in the text to figure out what else the author wants us to know.

So, read the text and then ask:

"What did the author want me to believe?"

"What was I supposed to find out?"

6 Monitoring

When we read, we should monitor our reading to make sure we understand what the author is saying, and have strategies to "fix" any comprehension problems as they arise. So, as you read the text, ask:

"Is this making sense?"
"Do I need to re-read?"
"Are there any text clues to help me fill in the missing information?"

7 Text Purpose

When we read, we should ask ourselves what the purpose of the text is. Did the author write to entertain the readers, to inform us about a particular topic, or to persuade the readers to think a certain way?
Read the text and then ask:
"What was the author's intention?"

8 Fact or Opinion?

When we read, we make judgements about what we are reading. We decide whether it is a fact or just an opinion and we should give reasons for our decision.
So, read the text and then ask:

"Is this a fact that can be proven?"
"Is this an opinion, someone's view?"

9 Visualising

When we read, we visualise what is happening while we read the text. Creating a movie in our minds helps us understand the setting, the characters and the events of the story.
So, read the text and then ask:

"Can I picture this new information?"
"What can I see, hear, smell or feel?"

10 Summarising

When we read, we summarise the information we are given.
To summarise, we identify the most important ideas in the text and explain them in our own words. So, read the text and then ask:

"What were the most important ideas?"

FICTION

The Worst Day

It was hot that day, too hot to do anything. The pool was green. Mum told Eliza that until Dad fixed it, which might be never, it was not fit to swim in. Dad was changing channels on the TV so quickly that no one could watch it. A Christmas beetle slowly lost its head in the loop of a rug, before Eliza was able to cut it free. Her father only laughed as she ran desperately around the house trying to find a pair of scissors while the beetle struggled to its death. Aunty Patsy stopped by and told Eliza she was growing up to look just like Barbara Streisand. Eliza knew that this was her aunt's way of telling her she had a big nose. To top it all off, her brother, Eric, blew his nose and then chased her around the house trying to rub his hanky in her face!

LITERAL COMPREHENSION

LITERAL COMPREHENSION

We understand what the text says. Understanding exactly what we have read is important so that we can then answer some questions about the text.

We can go back at any time to check what we understand.

We practise

What is the name of the girl who is having the worst day?	Eliza
What was wrong with the pool?	Pool was green
Who needed to fix it?	Eliza's dad
What happened to the Christmas beetle?	Died

Now that we understand what has been read, let's write a response in a full sentence using the questions ...

What is the name of the girl who is having the worst day?
The name of the girl having the worst day is Eliza.

What was wrong with the pool? The pool was green and was not fit to swim in.

Who needed to fix it? Eliza's dad needed to fix the pool.

What happened to the Christmas beetle?
The Christmas beetle lost its head in the loop of a rug and died.

Do you agree with the answers? Check the text to make sure.

INTERPRETIVE COMPREHENSION

INTERPRETIVE COMPREHENSION

We understand what the text says and then link information or ideas together to get a greater meaning. We can then answer some more questions about the text.

How was Eliza feeling?

Eliza felt like this was her worst day.

We can interpret this because that is the title of the story and the text tells us about all the terrible things that were happening to Eliza.

What did Eliza's father think about her attempt to save the beetle?

Eliza's father thought her attempt to save the beetle was funny.

We can interpret this because the text tells us *Her father only laughed as she ran desperately around the house trying to find a pair of scissors while the beetle struggled to its death.*

We can go back at any time to confirm what we understand.

Why did her brother chase her with his hanky?

Eliza's brother chased her with his hanky because he was teasing his sister.

We can interpret this because the text tells us that Eric *blew his nose and then chased her around the house trying to rub his hanky in her face!*

Did Eliza's father plan to fix the swimming pool?

Eliza's father did not plan to fix the swimming pool any time soon.

We can interpret this because the story tells us he was watching TV and Eliza's mother told her she could not go for a swim in the pool *until Dad fixed it, which might be never.*

Do you agree with the interpretations and the answers? Check the text to make sure.

APPLIED COMPREHENSION

We practise

APPLIED COMPREHENSION

We understand the text, then add what we have learned to what we already know and draw conclusions. We will be able to answer questions that go **beyond** the text.

Was Eliza's day really the worst day it could be?

Eliza's day was not really the worst day it could be because, although the events that happened were all annoying, they were not really that serious.

The title tells us that it was Eliza's worst day, but we know many other events could have occurred that would be more serious than what happened to Eliza on this day.

Were Eliza's parents worried about her having such a bad day?

Eliza's parents were not worried about her having her worst day.

We know this because the text tells us that her father was watching TV and did not help her with the pool, the beetle or her brother chasing her. We also know from the text that her mother was not worried because she didn't help Eliza in any way either.

Can you use what you already know to provide your own answers?

UNIT 1

SPIDER SOUP

Read this with a grown-up and discuss any tricky words.

FICTION

My pet spider's name is Webster. Webster loves eating lollies and chocolates. One day I gave Webster bubblegum to try. His legs got stuck together. He couldn't move. So I gave him a bath. I sat him on the soap and he slid into the water. He nearly drowned. Then I used Mum's hairdryer. I tried to blow his legs apart. Poor Webster flew into the kitchen and crash-landed in the butter. "Michael, get that spider out of here," Mum yelled.

Now Webster's legs were stuck together and he was covered in butter. I had to help him. I thought Webster must be hungry. He was in no state to catch a fly on his own. I left Webster on a plate in my room and went to catch some flies. It wasn't easy, until I took my shoes off. I made a discovery! Flies love smelly socks. I ran inside with flies all over my socks. "Webster," I called. "I've got some yummy lunch for you."

"Oh no!" I froze. Webster and the plate were gone. "Mum, where's the plate that was in my room?"
"I put it in the dishwasher," said Mum.
"Nooo!" I yelled. I opened the dishwasher. Two plates were stuck together. It had to be Webster and the bubblegum. Webster must have been squashed. A tear rolled down my face.

After school the next day I went straight home. I went to my room, shut the door and lay on my bed. I closed my eyes and thought about Webster.

"Aaaa!" Mum screamed.
I ran into the kitchen. "What's wrong, Mum?"
"Your spider was in my soup." Mum didn't look happy.

"Webster, you're alive!" I had a huge grin on my face. "Thanks, Mum."
Webster's legs were fine. The bubblegum was gone. I gave Webster a high-five. It was unreal to have him back.

***by Linda Stocks** (abridged)*

GLOSSARY

hungry	wanting food	**stuck**	not able to move
discovery	something found	**unreal**	fantastic

You practise

TOP TIP 1
What is the main idea?

1 What does the pet spider like to eat?

The spider likes to eat

2 What happened when Webster tried bubblegum?

3 How did Michael try to fix this?

4 Where was Webster finally found?

5 What started all the trouble with Webster?

6 Did Michael's mother like Webster?

7 Did Michael look after his pet spider well?

8 Did Michael love his pet spider?

9 Should pets eat human food?

10 Are spiders good pets to have?

FORGETFUL FRIDAY

Read this with a grown-up and discuss any tricky words.

FICTION

Some people love Fridays, but not Nelson. Friday was a day Nelson would rather forget. Friday was spelling test day. Every Friday, Nelson's brain liked to forget his spelling words.

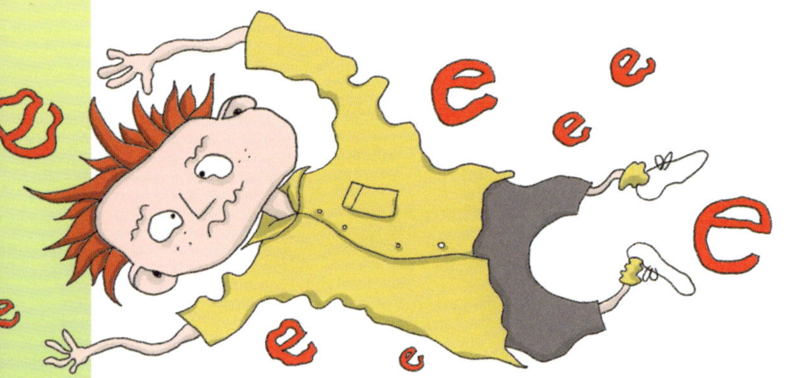

Miss Fazio handed out the spelling tests. Suddenly Ming let out a gasp. The whole class turned and looked. Ming began to sob. "I've forgotten where I put my glasses!" Ming cried.

"It's okay, Ming. We'll find them. Class, has anyone seen Ming's glasses?" asked Miss Fazio. Everyone shook their heads. "Right, check under your chairs for Ming's glasses," said Miss Fazio. Everyone looked but no one found Ming's glasses.

Ming started to cry again. "I can't do anything without them," she sobbed.

"Well they must be here somewhere," claimed Miss Fazio. "Everyone look for Ming's glasses."

Ming buried her head in her hands as the class searched around her. Leon found his old pencil case. Holly found her missing library book. Ruby found a hat. Nelson didn't find anything. He forgot all about looking and stared out the window. Ming was disappearing under a mountain of soggy tissues.

"Found them!" cried Brooke, holding up Ming's glasses. "You were sitting on them all along." Ming went bright red. Ming put them on.

The recess bell went, so everyone got up to go outside. "Forget it," said Miss Fazio, closing the door. "Stay in your seats. We have a spelling test to do!" Everyone groaned as they went back to their seats and did the test. For the first time ever Nelson got all his spelling words right. His brain had forgotten to forget!

It was a Friday that Nelson likes to remember and Ming likes to forget.

by Lisa Thompson *(abridged)*

GLOSSARY

forget	not be able to remember
sob	cry
forgotten	not remembered
groaned	made a sound when annoyed
remember	keep information in mind

We practise

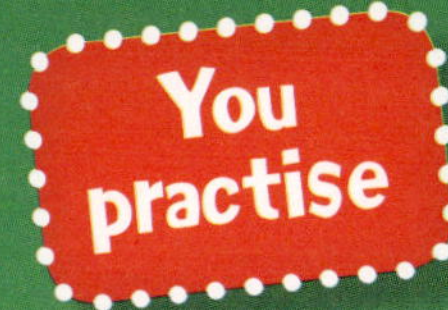

TOP TIP 2
Predict what happens next.

1 Who did not like Fridays?

The character who did not like Fridays was ______________________

2 Why was Ming crying?

____

3 What did the class have to do to help?

____

4 What happened when the bell went?

____

5 Was Miss Fazio a kind teacher?

____

6 Did Nelson work hard to remember his spelling words each week?

____

7 Was Ming worried about losing her glasses?

____

8 Is Nelson often forgetful?

____

9 Do you forget spelling you learn?

____

10 How do you think Nelson will go on next Friday's spelling test?

____

BOB time!

VOCABULARY 1

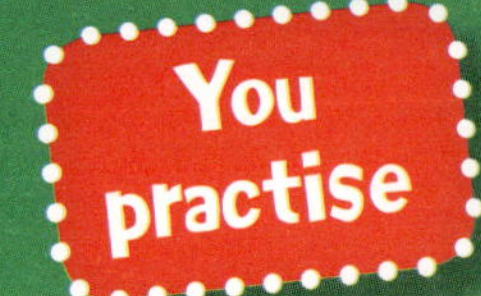

HIGH-FREQUENCY WORDS 1–20

The words featured in this unit are on the red word cards.

1 Words and meaning

For each word below, look at the shape, the sound blend and spelling. Write a sentence using the word.

get ______________________________

used ______________________________

also ______________________________

does ______________________________

help ______________________________

great ______________________________

should ______________________________

read ______________________________

sound ______________________________

show ______________________________

2 Fill the gaps

Write the correct words from the word bank to fill in the gaps.

through	me	around	part	put
tell	soup	last	below	large

a Let _______ know when you have _______ the books on the shelf.

b "Don't _______ anyone what my _______ in the play is," Hannah pleaded.

c The ball smashed ___________ the window and landed in the ___________.

d At ________ we went ________ the deck in the storm.

e The ________ gift had a red bow tied ____________ it.

BOB time!

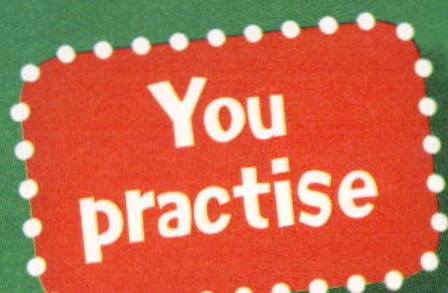

QUICK QUIZ 1

Unit 1 **Spider Soup** Unit 2 **Forgetful Friday**

1 Missing letters

Look at the word bank and fill in the missing letters in the words below.

butter	Friday	catch	spelling	gasp
drowned	hungry	plate	recess	groaned

a hun _ _ _

b gr _ a _ _ d

c _ _ id _ y

d dr _ _ _ ed

e c _ _ ch

f _ p _ ll _ _ _

g p _ _ te

h b _ tt _ _

i g _ s _

j re _ _ _ s

2 Word pictures

Draw a picture to illustrate each word and then copy the word under your picture.

brain	lollies	chocolates	kitchen	window
________	________	________	________	________
flies	spider	tissues	chairs	glasses
________	________	________	________	________

BOB time!

UNIT 5

TAKE ME TO YOUR LEADER

Read this with a grown-up and discuss any tricky words.

FICTION

Tim wakes up. Saturday! In the fridge is the lovely jelly he made last night. This is going to be a great day. Thump. Tim frowns. Thump. It's coming from the wardrobe. Tim slides the door open. A tiny purple alien steps out.

"Take me to your weader!" The alien is only as big as a teddy bear but he has a zap gun.

"I am taking over your pwanet. Give up!" the alien squeaks. He fires his zap gun at Tim's elbow.

"Ow! Stop it!"

"Your pwanet is taken over!" the alien squeaks.

"How many of you are there?" Tim asks.

"One."

Tim laughs. "You? You're too little!"

Gweep rubs his three foreheads. "Me in BIG twouble. This is the sixth pwanet me NOT taken over," Gweep moans.

"Sorry," Tim says.

"If you really sorry, you will talk to boss. You say, 'Gweep take over my pwanet. He very good at it.' Gweep be very happy."

Tim shrugs, "Okay."

Gweep runs to the wardrobe. There stands a tiny, shiny spaceship. "Come in!"

Tim shakes his head, "I can't fit in there."

"Maybe I just take your head," says Gweep.

"No. Wait here," says Tim. Tim runs to the kitchen, grabs the jelly and takes it back to the alien. "Here is some lime jelly instead."

Gweep looks at the wobbly green jelly. "It's saying no."

"It isn't saying no. It's shaking because it is scared of you. Take it back to your boss. Tell him you have taken over the slime on Earth."

Gweep laughs as he snatches the bowl, runs into the spaceship and slams the door. The wardrobe rumbles and shakes. Then the spaceship is gone.

All week Tim wonders about Gweep. What happened to him? On Friday, Tim helps unpack the shopping; there is a new brand of jelly. Tim smiles as he reads the label — Gweep's Galactic Jelly, Slime Surprise Flavour.

by Bren MacDibble (abridged)

GLOSSARY

alien	creature from outer space
forehead	part of face above eyebrows
wardrobe	cupboard where clothes are kept
rumbles	low grumbling noises

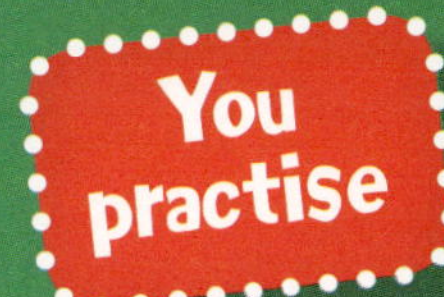

TOP TIP 3
Think about cause and effect.
What happened?
What caused it?

LITERAL

What is the name of the alien?

The name of the alien is

What weapon does the alien have?

How many planets has the alien tried to take over?

What did the alien take back to his boss?

INTERPRETIVE

Was Tim helpful to the alien?

Was Tim scared of the alien?

How did Tim trick Gweep with the jelly?

Was Gweep happy when he went home in his spaceship?

APPLIED

Was Gweep's journey successful?

What do you think happened when Gweep got back to his planet?

BOB time!

THING IN THE FRIDGE

Read this with a grown-up and discuss any tricky words.

FICTION

It all began when someone turned the power off by mistake. In the freezer the ice-cream melted. The pet food dribbled. Everything got mixed up in a slimy lake. Strange blobs began to grow. In one of

these blobs, Thing was born. She was white, like the ice-cream, and covered in grey fuzz.

Suddenly, the freezer door opened. She hid.

"Pew! Pong! Who turned off the power?" yelled an angry voice. Thing stayed hiding. Slam! The door shut.

"Hey! Let me out! It's really cold in here!" said a buzzy voice in the dark. A fly was trapped in the freezer. "Help! I wanted the fridge, not the freezer. All the best stuff is down below – sausages, cheese," he croaked. "Down below" sounded like a great place to Thing! She hopped down to the freezer door and waited. Soon enough, the door opened and Thing slid down an icicle onto a tray of soft, pink sausages. She ate some. "Now, I want to find the cheese."

"Cheese?" growled a thick voice. "Did someone say cheeeeeese?" A fat, yellow shape slid off a shelf. It had a big mouth with sharp teeth and it stank. "Do you want cheese with bite?" the Blob said. The Blob rushed at Thing and knocked her over. Thing grabbed a carrot and swung it at the Blob. The Blob chased Thing with growls and snaps. But brave Thing would not stop.

Just then, the door opened and the Blob and Thing fell out. Thing landed safely and hid under the fridge. But the Blob hit the kitchen floor hard. Splat! Thing picked up a small piece of the Blob that had landed under the fridge. She put it in her mouth. "Wow! So this is cheese. I love it! I love smelly cheese!" she shouted.

After that, Thing didn't live in the fridge. Instead, she stayed under the fridge. She made friends with the mice, who always shared their cheese.

by Susan Knight (abridged)

We practise

GLOSSARY

mistake	accidental error	**icicle**	frozen drops of water
slimy	like thin sticky mud	**stank**	smelled bad

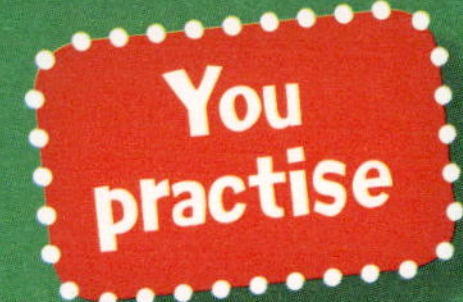

TOP TIP 4
Make connections between what you read and what you know.

LITERAL

How did this story begin?

This story began

Where was Thing born?

Who was the visitor in the freezer?

What happened when Thing first found the Blob?

INTERPRETIVE

Why did Thing hide?

Was the Blob a bully? Explain how you know.

Was Thing brave? Explain how you know.

How did Thing's life change?

APPLIED

Does a bully win in the end?

Is making new friends a good idea?

BOB time!

VOCABULARY 2

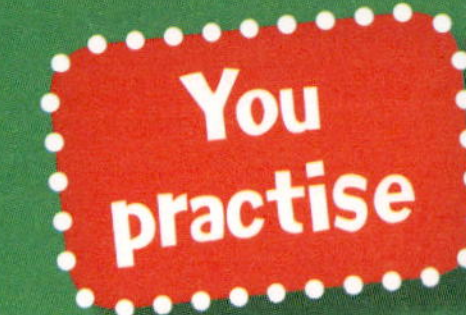

HIGH-FREQUENCY WORDS 21–40

The words featured in this unit are on the blue word cards.

Syllables

Words are made up of sound "chunks", or syllables.
Write the words below showing their syllables and the number of syllables in each word, for example some / thing (2).

a back ______________________

b often ______________________

c even ______________________

d another ______________________

e different ______________________

f never ______________________

g years ______________________

h something ______________________

i together ______________________

j man ______________________

Alphabetical order

Write the words from the word bank in alphabetical order.

men	home	saw	much	too
came	place	say	big	us

a big

b ______________________

c ______________________

d ______________________

e ______________________

f ______________________

g ______________________

h ______________________

i ______________________

j ______________________

BOB time!

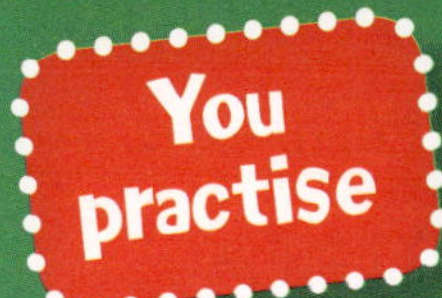

QUICK QUIZ 2

Unit 5 Take Me to Your Leader Unit 6 Thing in the Fridge

1 Nouns and adjectives

For each noun in the word bank, choose an interesting adjective to describe it. For each adjective, choose a noun to follow it.

Saturday	purple	alien	shiny	beam
forehead	planet	spaceship	kitchen	new

sunny Saturday ____________ purple socks ____________

____________ ____________

____________ ____________

____________ ____________

____________ ____________

2 Fill the blanks

Fill in the blanks in the passage using these words.

cheese	scraped	melted	sausages	friends
power	vegetables	mistake	mice	freezer

It was a ____________ to go out into the cold morning. It was like stepping into a ____________! The snow was like powder but it soon ____________. My ____________ and I had a fire in the cabin – it used electric ____________ but it still looked real! We ____________ the snow off our boots and I barbequed some ____________, while Nina cooked the ____________. We nibbled on ____________ and crackers while we cooked. I was amazed that even in this cold weather there were ____________ scampering about!

BOB time!

FACING FEARS

Read this with a grown-up and discuss any tricky words.

FICTION

Bruno stood frozen in the playground. A bee buzzed around him. Buzz buzz. Only Bruno's eyes moved, watching the bee. If there was one thing Bruno was afraid of it was bees. Leon saw Bruno standing like a statue. He called to Miles. They watched Bruno and the bee. Beatrice and Brooke joined them. So did Heeni, Ruby and Holly.

"What's everyone looking at?" asked Nelson, joining the crowd.

"Bruno has a bee buzzing around him," whispered Ruby.

"So?" snorted Nelson. "It's just a bee."

"Bruno is afraid of bees," said Miles. Nelson laughed so hard it hurt.

"Shhh!" said Ruby. "You'll make the bee angry!"

Nelson rolled his eyes. "Has anyone noticed how big Bruno is and how small that bee is?"

No one was listening to Nelson. Everyone was staring at Bruno and the bee. Bruno's eyes were wide with fear. His heart was racing. The bee landed on Bruno's nose. Bruno fainted.

When Bruno woke, the bee was gone. Instead, 11 heads hovered above him. One of the heads belonged to Miss Fazio. "He's awake," she declared. "Give him some room." Miss Fazio helped Bruno to his feet. Bruno felt his nose.

"It didn't sting me!" he said amazed.

"Maybe the bee was scared of you," said Holly.

"Nah," said Nelson, "I bet it's gone back to tell the other bees at the hive how sweet you smell. Soon it will be back with its friends, hunting for you." Bruno's legs went wobbly.

"That's enough, Nelson," said Miss Fazio. "Bruno, you are fine. The bee has gone. There's no need to be afraid of bees. They're wonderful creatures."

"They sting," reminded Bruno.

"That one didn't," said Ruby.

"Not all bees sting," said Miss Fazio. "A bee will only sting you if it feels in danger. Perhaps you should learn more about bees, Bruno, and then you won't be afraid of them any more."

by Lisa Thompson (abridged)

We practise

GLOSSARY

statue a 3D artwork usually made of stone or metal

hovering staying in one place above the ground

hive a place where bees live

wonderful great, fantastic, terrific

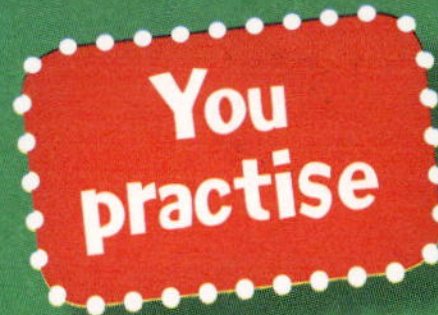

TOP TIP 5
Use clues to infer what else the author is saying.

LITERAL

1. Why was Bruno standing frozen in the playground?

Bruno was standing frozen because

2. What was the one thing Bruno was afraid of?

3. Where did the bee land?

4. What happened when the bee landed?

INTERPRETIVE

5. Why did Nelson tease Bruno?

6. Why did Miss Fazio stop Nelson from teasing Bruno any further?

7. Why do you think Bruno was afraid of bees?

8. How did Miss Fazio try to stop Bruno from feeling afraid of bees?

APPLIED

9. Will finding out more about what you are afraid of help?

10. Why is "Facing Fears" a good title for the story?

BOB time!

NON-FICTION

Redback Spiders

Female redback spiders are usually black with a red or orange stripe on their backs. They are about one centimetre in size. Male redback spiders are usually light brown with white markings on their backs. They are about four millimetres in size. Redback spiders live all over Australia and love areas where they can find food and shelter, and where it is warm enough for them to breed. They love living among rocks, and in logs, shrubs, sheds, bins and garages. Their webs are shaped like a funnel. They eat insects and are able to capture large insects such as crickets in their sticky webs.

LITERAL COMPREHENSION

We understand what the text says. Understanding exactly what we have read is important so that we can then answer some questions about the text.

We can go back at any time to check what we understand.

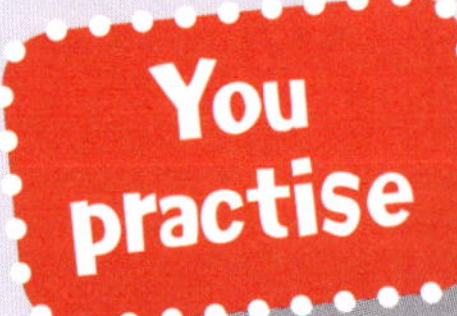

What colour stripe do female redback spiders have?

Female redback spiders have a red or orange stripe on their backs.

Which spider is bigger, the male or the female redback spider?

The female redback spider is bigger then the male.

Where do redback spiders live in Australia?

Redback spiders live all over Australia.

What shape is a redback spider's web?

The redback spider's web is shaped like a funnel.

Do you agree with the answers? Check the text to make sure.

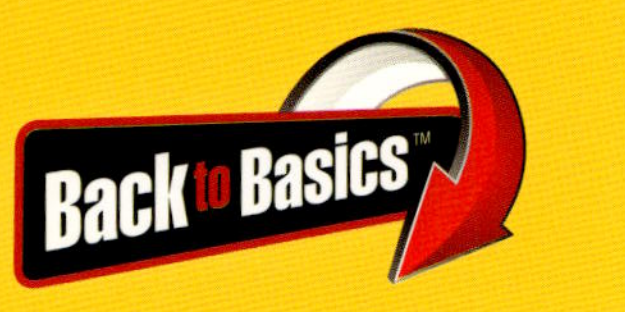

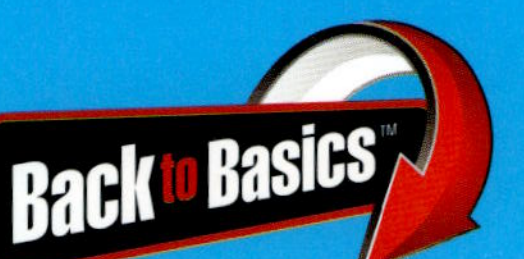

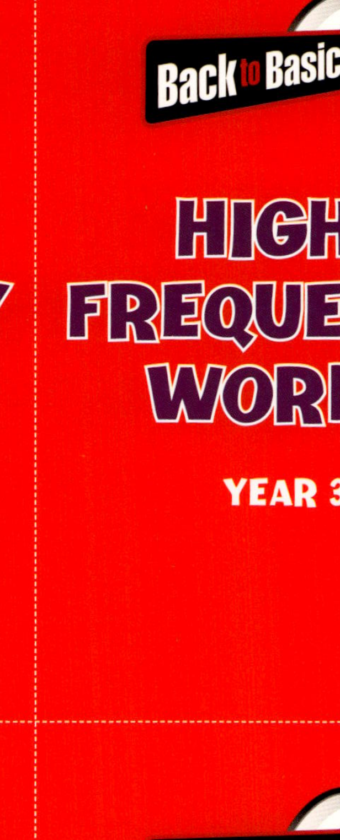
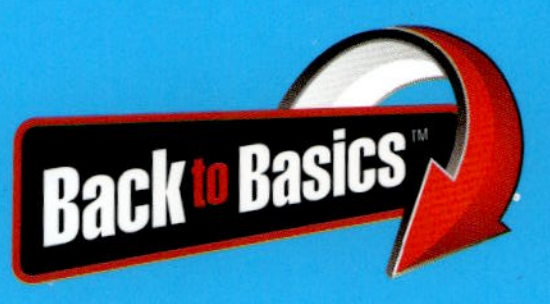

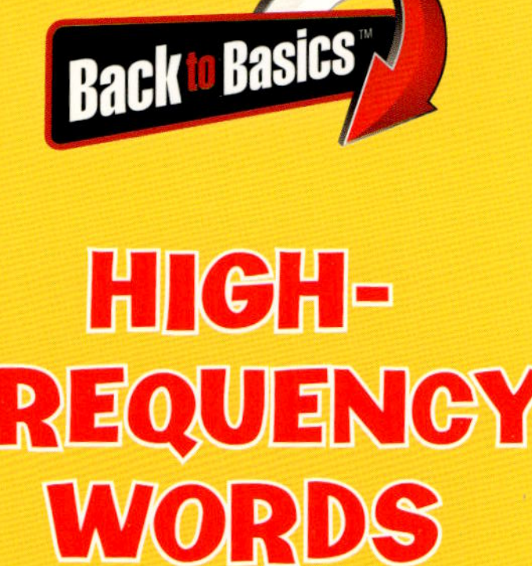
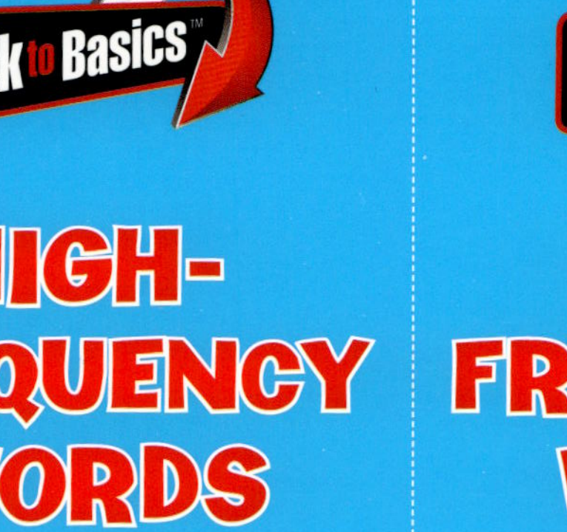

Back to Basics™

HIGH-FREQUENCY WORDS

YEAR 3

Back to Basics™
HIGH-FREQUENCY WORDS
YEAR 3
Back to Basics™
HIGH-FREQUENCY WORDS
YEAR 3
Back to Basics™
HIGH-FREQUENCY WORDS
YEAR 3
Back to Basics™
HIGH-FREQUENCY WORDS
YEAR 3
Back to Basics™
HIGH-FREQUENCY WORDS
YEAR 3
Back to Basics™
HIGH-FREQUENCY WORDS
YEAR 3
Back to Basics™
HIGH-FREQUENCY WORDS
YEAR 3
Back to Basics™
HIGH-FREQUENCY WORDS
YEAR 3
Back to Basics™
HIGH-FREQUENCY WORDS
YEAR 3

1 get
2 used
3 also
4 does
5 help

6 great
7 should
8 read
9 sound
10 show

11 through
12 me
13 around
14 part
15 put

16 tell
17 soup
18 last
19 below
20 large

21 back
22 often
23 even
24 another
25 different

26 never
27 years
28 something
29 together
30 man

31 men
32 home
33 saw
34 much
35 too

36 came
37 place
38 say
39 big
40 us

41 before
42 small
43 go
44 every
45 any

46 give
47 day
48 air
49 come
50 left

51 work
52 end
53 well
54 thought
55 such

56 both
57 away
58 asked
59 again
60 house

61 good
62 same
63 three
64 here
65 off

66 found
67 line
68 along
69 few
70 world

71 new
72 right
73 word
74 take
75 went

76 still
77 set
78 while
79 those
80 bent

81 write
82 look
83 must
84 why
85 old

86 between
87 own
88 might
89 always
90 going

91 our
92 think
93 because
94 things
95 number

96 name
97 under
98 next
99 looked
100 want

HIGH-FREQUENCY WORDS

YEAR 3

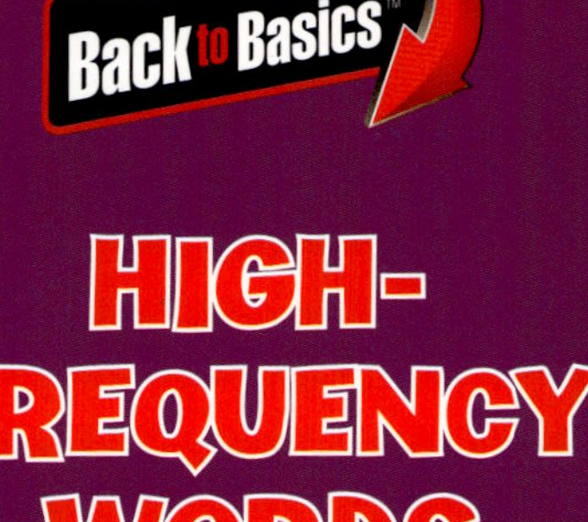

HIGH-FREQUENCY WORDS

YEAR 3

HIGH-FREQUENCY WORDS

YEAR 3

HIGH-FREQUENCY WORDS

YEAR 3

HIGH-FREQUENCY WORDS

YEAR 3

HIGH-FREQUENCY WORDS

YEAR 3

Back to Basics™

HIGH-FREQUENCY WORDS

YEAR 3

HIGH-FREQUENCY WORDS

YEAR 3

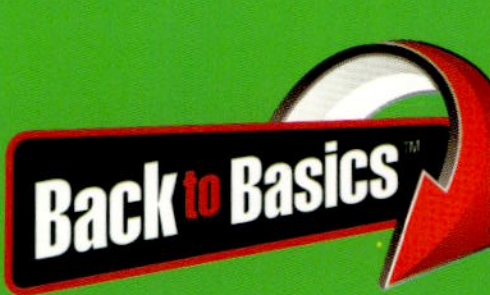

HIGH-FREQUENCY WORDS

YEAR 3

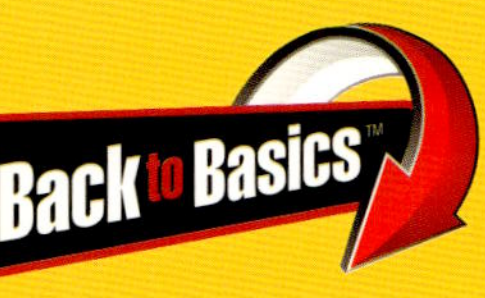

HIGH-FREQUENCY WORDS

YEAR 3

INTERPRETIVE COMPREHENSION

INTERPRETIVE COMPREHENSION

We understand what the text says and then link information or ideas together to get a greater meaning. We can then answer some more questions about the text.

Would the female spider be stronger than the male?

The female redback spider would be stronger because it is bigger.

We can interpret this because the text says that the female is about one centimetre and the male is only four millimetres. Because she is bigger, she is likely to also be stronger.

Would redback spiders like to live in a compost bin?

Redback spiders would like to live in a compost bin because they would have warmth, shelter and food.

We can interpret this because the text tells us *redback spiders love areas where they can find food and shelter, and where it is warm enough for them to breed.*

Do redback spiders eat flies?

Yes, redback spiders do eat flies.

We can interpret this because the text tells us *They eat insects.* We know redback spiders eat insects, so, as flies are insects, redback spiders would eat flies.

Do you agree with the interpretations and the answers? Check the text to make sure.

We can go back at any time to confirm what we understand.

APPLIED COMPREHENSION

APPLIED COMPREHENSION

We understand the text, then add what we have learned to what we already know and draw conclusions. We will be able to answer questions that go **beyond** the text.

Why is the redback spider's web shaped like a funnel?

The redback spider's web is shaped like a funnel so that insects think it is a big hole. They get trapped as they go into the tunnel with its sticky web.

The text tells us that the web is shaped like a funnel and that it is sticky, so we can use what we know about funnels and about sticky material to answer the question.

Why would redback spiders live where humans live?

Redback spiders live where humans live because there are lots of places to shelter, such as sheds, bins and garages. Humans also attract other insects – and, where insects are, redback spiders want to be too!

The text tells us some places redback spiders like to live and what they like to eat, and we know that humans create the kinds of shelter redbacks like. We also know there are always insects around us – so it makes sense that redback spiders would live around us too.

Can you use what you already know to provide your own answers?

POLAR EXPLORERS

Read this with a grown-up and discuss any tricky words.

NON-FICTION

Explorers have been excited by the polar regions of Antarctica and the Arctic for hundreds of years.

The main goals of early Arctic exploration were to chart and navigate the Arctic's coastlines and islands, study the region and to be the first to reach the North Pole.

Although people have lived in the Arctic for thousands of years, Antarctica was not seen by humans until 1820. From then, many countries sent expeditions to Antarctica. They carried out scientific research, claimed land and mapped the continent. They also competed to be the first to reach the South Pole.

Arctic and Antarctic explorers experienced many hardships and dangers. They battled blizzards, frostbite, hunger, homesickness, exhaustion and cramped living spaces. They risked injury, sickness and even death.

Today, many scientists live and work in the polar regions. Tourists can also visit Antarctica.

GLOSSARY

exploration the search of unknown areas
Arctic most northerly part of the Earth
Antarctica most southerly part of the Earth
chart to make a map of
navigate to find a way to reach a destination
expeditions trips to search
hardships difficult times
frostbite frozen skin of fingers, toes, ears, nose
exhaustion state of being very tired

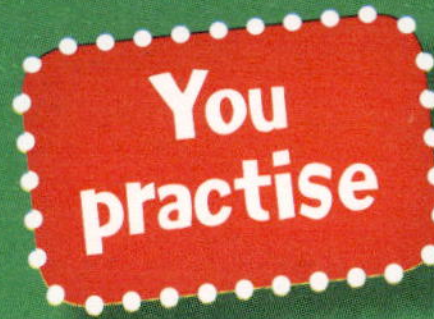

TOP TIP 6
Monitor your reading to make sure you understand.

LITERAL

How long have explorers been interested in the polar regions?

Explorers have been interested in the polar regions

What were the main goals of early Arctic exploration?

When was Antarctica first seen by humans?

Why did many countries send expeditions to Antarctica?

INTERPRETIVE

Was exploration hard on the explorers?

Can people live in the Arctic?

What types of people choose to go to the polar regions?

Why do explorers risk their lives to explore the polar regions?

APPLIED

Why did countries try to be first to reach the North and South poles?

Why do people find the North and South poles so interesting?

BOB time!

VOCABULARY 3

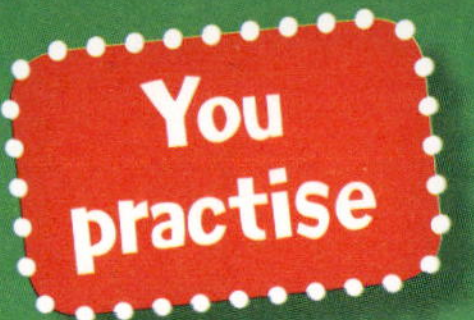

HIGH-FREQUENCY WORDS 41–60

The words featured in this unit are on the yellow word cards.

Scrambled words

Unscramble each of these words from the word bank and then write it in a sentence.

before	any	come	well	away
small	give	left	thought	asked
go	day	work	such	again
every	air	end	both	house

a ywaa ______________________

b slmal ______________________

c boerfe ______________________

d omec ______________________

e thguoth ______________________

f nya ______________________

g ftel ______________________

h seadk ______________________

i lwle ______________________

j geiv ______________________

60-second challenge

In 60 seconds write out as many words as you can from the word bank. Try again to improve your score.

____

____

____

BOB time!

You practise

QUICK QUIZ 3

Unit 9 **Facing Fears** Unit 10 **Polar Explorers**

1 Sentence jumble

Rewrite these jumbled sentences correctly and underline the words that are from the word bank.

playground	watching	statue	looking	afraid
bees	angry	fear	heart	nose

a dark the I afraid of am.

____

b live a Bees hive in.

____

c playground in after meet Let's school the.

____

d pumps The body around heart the blood.

____

e heights is fear of A vertigo called.

____

Word frames

Find a word from the word bank to fit each word frame and write the letters in the boxes.

explorers	polar	thousands	years	humans
countries	claimed	mapped	hardship	dangers

a

b

c

d

e

BOB time!

TECHNOLOGICAL WONDERS

Read this with a grown-up and discuss any tricky words.

The Boeing 747 aircraft was a revolution in air travel. Introduced in 1970, it could carry almost three times more people than any other aircraft of the time.

The number of people using air travel increased during the 1960s. Boeing, an American aircraft manufacturer, was asked by Pan Am to build a large passenger aircraft.

Even before the first 747 was ready for testing, 26 airlines had ordered the aircraft. The first commercial flight of the Boeing 747, from New York to London, was on 22 January 1970.

Several versions of the 747 have been produced since 1970. By 1990, Boeing was producing a new 747 every six days. Each version increased the range of earlier versions. The freighter version of the 747 has a hinged nose to allow cargo loading through the front of the aircraft. Nearly 300 of these aircraft carry half of the world's air cargo.

The Airbus A380 is now the world's largest passenger aircraft, but the Boeing 747 is still being made. It remains the fastest subsonic passenger aircraft, cruising at 85.5 per cent of the speed of sound.

GLOSSARY

revolution big change
manufacturer maker of a product
versions different forms of the same thing
freighter machine to transport large items
hinged allowing something to open and close
range distance an aircraft can fly
cargo items to be transported
subsonic slower than the speed of sound

You practise

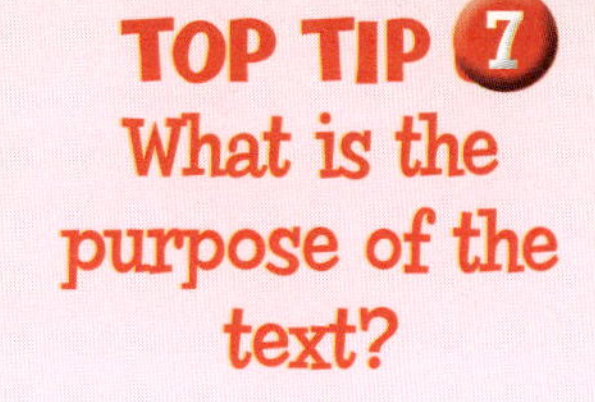

LITERAL

1. What year was the Boeing 747 introduced?

The Boeing 747 was introduced

2. How many people could the Boeing 747 carry when it was introduced?

3. How many airlines had ordered the 747 even before it had been tested?

4. By 1990 how often were Boeing 747s being produced?

INTERPRETIVE

5. What was special about the freighter version of the 747?

6. Why is the Airbus A380 used for popular flights?

7. What is special about the Boeing 747s being made today?

8. Why do we want an aircraft to fly at such great speed?

APPLIED

9. Will the Airbus A380 remain the world's largest aircraft?

10. Why would we want bigger, faster planes?

BOB time!

UNIT 14

THE HUMAN BODY

Read this with a grown-up and discuss any tricky words.

NON-FICTION

The human body is a collection of organ systems. Each one has a job to do to keep the body working and healthy.

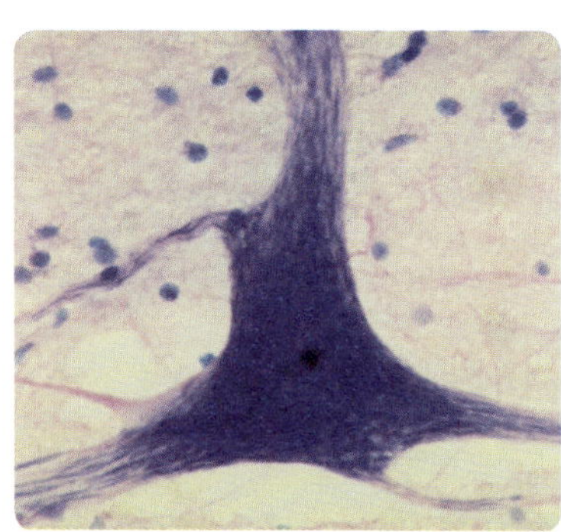

These organ systems are made entirely of fluids, cells and the product of cells (what cells make).

Cells

Cells are the basic building blocks of life. Some are strong, such as cells in bone, and some send electrical messages, like those in the brain.

Cells that have similar functions are organised in groups and layers called tissues. Cells can reproduce, making the new cells needed for growth and the replacement of damaged tissues.

Organs

Groups of tissues form the organs, such as the skin, liver and heart. Organs are arranged into organ systems. For example, the stomach, liver and small intestine are organs of the digestive system.

There are organ systems for protecting the body from disease and getting rid of waste. Other organ systems allow the body to breathe, move and reproduce.

GLOSSARY

organ	internal body part with a particular job to do, such as liver, heart, brain
entirely	completely
reproduce	make more
replacement	making of another when one is lost or damaged
damaged	needing repair
system	where one part works with another part
disease	sickness
waste	what your body does not need

You practise

TOP TIP 8
Decide if what you've read is fact or opinion.

LITERAL

1. Why does the body have organ systems?

The body has organ systems to

2. Where can you find cells that are strong?

3. Where can you find cells that send electrical messages?

4. What do groups of cells with a similar function form?

INTERPRETIVE

5. What can cells do if tissue is damaged?

6. What are three organs that help us to use the food we eat?

7. What kinds of electrical messages would the brain receive?

8. Why is the skin the body's largest organ?

APPLIED

9. If we did not have one cell to start with, would we be born?

10. Without organ systems could we live?

BOB time!

VOCABULARY 4

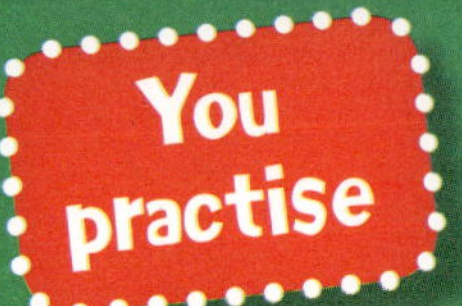

HIGH-FREQUENCY WORDS 61–80

The words featured in this unit are on the green word cards.

1 Asking questions

Each of these words finishes with a question mark. What could the question be? Write questions using each of the words.

good?	same?	three?	here?	off?
found?	line?	along?	few?	world?

Here's an example: Was the dog found?

2 Crosswords

Find pairs of words in the list that have a common letter in them and write them so they criss-cross.

new	right	word	take	went
still	set	while	those	bent

Here's an example:

```
  t
  h
w o r d
  s
  e
```


BOB time!

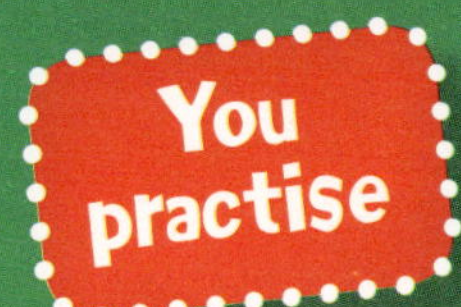

QUICK QUIZ 4

Unit 13 Technological Wonders Unit 14 The Human Body

1 Spelling mistakes

Find the words spelled incorrectly in these sentences and rewrite them correctly.

aircraft	travel	build	large	passenger
producing	cargo	cruising	speed	sound

a "Let's biuld a sand castle," Jake said to Ellie. __________

b Qantas aircarft all have the flying kangaroo logo. __________

c The yacht went criusing around Sydney Harbour. __________

d "What's that spooky sownd?" Gwen gasped. __________

e The huge ship unloaded its cargoe onto the dock. __________

f When I grow up I want to travell the world! __________

g Oliver's larj suitcase went missing at the airport. __________

h The students are predusing excellent work. __________

i It is very dangerous to speeed when driving. __________

j The plane waited for the last pasenger to board. __________

2 Creative writing

Write each word below in a creative, unusual and colourful way.

human	body	life	growth	organs
skin	liver	heart	stomach	cells

____

____

____

BOB time!

OUR FUTURE IN SPACE

Read this with a grown-up and discuss any tricky words.

NON-FICTION

There is very little gravity in space, so it is known as microgravity. This means that when astronauts are in orbit things are done differently from the way they are done on Earth.

Food is mainly dehydrated or heat-stabilised. Drinks are also dehydrated. When food has been rehydrated and heated, astronauts eat the food on magnetic trays. The magnetic tray means that the knives, forks and spoons stick to the trays and don't float away. The food has some moisture, so it sticks to the spoon. A straw is used for drinks.

Astronauts sleep in sleeping bags attached to the walls of the station. They zip themselves in so that they don't float out of the bag while asleep. It is very important that astronauts sleep near a ventilation fan, which keeps air moving. This is because warm air does not rise in space. Without a fan the astronauts would be surrounded by carbon dioxide that they have exhaled and would not get enough oxygen.

The space station has treadmills and exercise bikes. Lower back and leg muscles aren't used much in space, so astronauts need to do hours of exercise each day to stop muscles losing tone and mass. Astronauts need to be strapped onto the equipment so they don't float away.

GLOSSARY

gravity	a force that pulls towards Earth
orbit	circular movement around a planet
dehydrated	all moisture taken out
ventilation	introduction of fresh air
carbon dioxide	gas that humans breathe out
exhaled	breathed out
oxygen	gas that humans breathe in

You practise

TOP TIP 9
Create visual images of what you read.

1. How do astronauts eat their food?

   Astronauts eat their food

2. Where do astronauts sleep?

3. Why do astronauts need a ventilation fan?

4. Why do astronauts need to exercise?

5. Is there any gravity in a space station?

6. Would astronauts float around rather than walk?

7. Would exercise equipment need to be attached to the space station?

8. Do astronauts need strong muscles before entering a space station?

9. Where do astronauts get oxygen from if there are no plants in space?

10. Do astronauts need to train before going to a space station?

BOB time!

LIFE ON THE GOLDFIELDS

Read this with a grown-up and discuss any tricky words.

Life on the goldfields was cramped, dirty and often violent. Very few miners found the gold they dreamed of.

Miners lived in tents and often didn't have enough food. Dirty living conditions and poor nutrition meant diseases spread easily. The work was also hard and dangerous. Underground mines could collapse and bury diggers.

Many foreigners who arrived were British but there were also American, French, Italian, German, Polish and Hungarian miners. More than 40 000 Chinese immigrants worked on the Australian goldfields.

Miners paid a monthly fee of 30 shillings (about a week's wage) for the right to dig a few square metres of land. They could keep any gold they found. The police often fought with miners who had not paid their fees.

Over the years, life on the goldfields improved. From 1851 to 1871, the Australian population grew from 430 000 to more than one million people. Melbourne became the main entry port to the Victorian goldfields. It developed into Australia's largest city and financial centre.

By the late 19th century, large, busy towns such as Ballarat, Bendigo and Kalgoorlie surrounded the goldfields. People built houses, shops and hotels. Music, theatre and sport added to goldfield life.

GLOSSARY

cramped	squashed
nutrition	health quality of food
collapse	fall down
foreigners	people from other countries
immigrants	people who come to live in another country
fee	cost to do something
port	where boats can dock

TOP TIP 10
Summarise the most important ideas.

How could life on the goldfields be described?

Life on the goldfields was

What were the miners living conditions like?

Why was the work of mining dangerous?

What were some of the nationalities of the foreign miners?

Was the fee to mine expensive?

Did all miners pay their fees?

Why did Melbourne grow so quickly?

How did life for the miners improve?

Why did miners put up with living in such poor conditions?

What would happen to the miners who did not find gold?

VOCABULARY 5

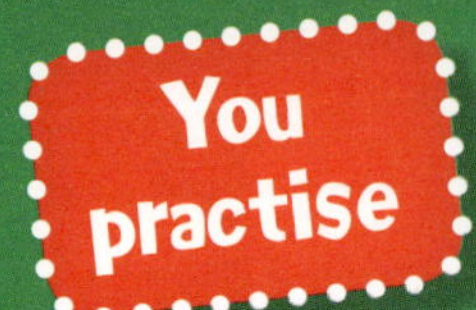

HIGH-FREQUENCY WORDS 81–100

The words featured in this unit are on the purple word cards.

Word graphs

Look at the number of letters in these words and write them where they fit into each bar of the graph below.

write	look	must	why	old
between	own	might	always	going

a b c d e f g h i j

Sentences

Try to put all ten words in one sentence that makes sense. Good luck!

our	think	because	things	number
name	under	next	looked	want

BOB time!

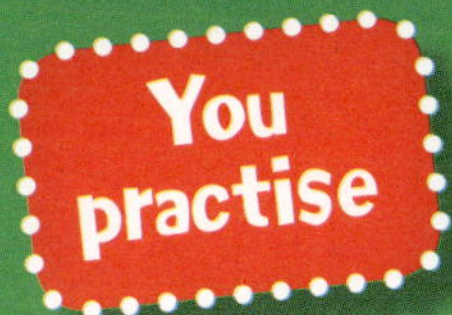

QUICK QUIZ 5

Unit 17 **Our Future in Space** Unit 18 **Life on the Goldfields**

Spellcheckers

Spellcheckers on computers read the words and decide if any letters have been used incorrectly. Then they correct the spelling for you. Be a spellchecker for these words.

gravity space astronauts orbit Earth
sleeping float asleep station exercising

a orbet		f astronants	
b asliep		g Erthe	
c fluat		h gravety	
d sleiping		i spase	
e staiton		j exersising	

Word pictures

Create a snake by adding these words behind the snake's head.

goldfields cramped dirty violent miners

Create a trail of ants by adding these words behind the ant.

dreamed tents diseases dangerous collapse

BOB time!

TEST 1

FICTION: RESTRUCTURING THE TEXT

★ Turn back to Unit 1 on page 10 and re-read Spider Soup.
★ The text below is out of sequence. Put the paragraphs back in order by writing the paragraph numbers in the correct order in the boxes below.

☐ ☐ ☐ ☐ ☐ ☐

Spider Soup

1 "Oh no!" I froze. Webster and the plate were gone. "Mum, where's the plate that was in my room?"
"I put it in the dishwasher," said Mum.
"Nooo!" I yelled. I opened the dishwasher. Two plates were stuck together. It had to be Webster and the bubblegum. Webster must have been squashed. A tear rolled down my face.

2 After school the next day I went straight home. I went to my room, shut the door and lay on my bed. I closed my eyes and thought about Webster.

3 "Webster, you're alive!" I had a huge grin on my face. "Thanks, Mum." Webster's legs were fine. The bubblegum was gone. I gave Webster a high-five. It was unreal to have him back.

4 My pet spider's name is Webster. Webster loves eating lollies and chocolates. One day I gave Webster bubblegum to try. His legs got stuck together. He couldn't move. So I gave him a bath. I sat him on the soap and he slid into the water. He nearly drowned. Then I used Mum's hairdryer. I tried to blow his legs apart. Poor Webster flew into the kitchen and crash-landed in the butter.
"Michael, get that spider out of here," Mum yelled.

5 "Aaaa!" Mum screamed.
I ran into the kitchen. "What's wrong, Mum?"
"Your spider was in my soup." Mum didn't look happy.

6 Now Webster's legs were stuck together and he was covered in butter. I had to help him. I thought Webster must be hungry. He was in no state to catch a fly on his own. I left Webster on a plate in my room and went to catch some flies. It wasn't easy, until I took my shoes off. I made a discovery! Flies love smelly socks. I ran inside with flies all over my socks. "Webster," I called. "I've got some yummy lunch for you."

BOB time!

TEST 2

NON-FICTION: RESTRUCTURING THE TEXT

★ Turn back to Unit 18 on page 38 and re-read Life on the Goldfields.

★ The following text is out of sequence. Put the paragraphs back in order by writing the paragraph numbers in the correct order in the boxes below.

☐ ☐ ☐ ☐ ☐ ☐

Life on the Goldfields

1 Many foreigners who arrived were British but there were also American, French, Italian, German, Polish and Hungarian miners. More than 40 000 Chinese immigrants worked on the Australian goldfields.

2 Life on the goldfields was cramped, dirty and often violent. Very few miners found the gold they dreamed of.

3 Miners paid a monthly fee of 30 shillings (about a week's wage) for the right to dig a few square metres of land. They could keep any gold they found. The police often fought with miners who had not paid their fees.

4 By the late 19th century, large, busy towns such as Ballarat, Bendigo and Kalgoorlie surrounded the goldfields. People built houses, shops and hotels. Music, theatre and sport added to goldfield life.

5 Miners lived in tents and often didn't have enough food. Dirty living conditions and poor nutrition meant diseases spread easily. The work was also hard and dangerous. Underground mines could collapse and bury diggers.

6 Over the years, life on the goldfields improved. From 1851 to 1871, the Australian population grew from 430 000 to more than one million people. Melbourne became the main entry port to the Victorian goldfields. It developed into Australia's largest city and financial centre.

BOB time!

HIGH-FREQUENCY WORDS

Ask an adult to read you the high-frequency words in blocks of 20 and write each word in its correct box. Start with the red cards (words 1–20), then the blue cards (words 21–40), the yellow cards (words 41–60), the green cards (words 61–80) and finally the purple cards (words 81–100).

1	21	41	61	81
2	22	42	62	82
3	23	43	63	83
4	24	44	64	84
5	25	45	65	85
6	26	46	66	86
7	27	47	67	87
8	28	48	68	88
9	29	49	69	89
10	30	50	70	90
11	31	51	71	91
12	32	52	72	92
13	33	53	73	93
14	34	54	74	94
15	35	55	75	95
16	36	56	76	96
17	37	57	77	97
18	38	58	78	98
19	39	59	79	99
20	40	60	80	100

ANSWERS

Unit 1 – Spider Soup

1. The pet spider likes to eat lollies and chocolates.
2. When Webster tried bubblegum his legs got stuck together.
3. Webster's owner gave him a bath to try to fix his sticky legs.
4. Webster was finally found in Mum's bowl of soup.
5. All the trouble started when Webster was given bubblegum to eat.
6. Answers may vary. No, Michael's mother didn't like Webster because she shouted when he landed in the butter and screamed when she found him in her soup.
7. Answers may vary. No, Michael didn't look after Webster very well because he fed him the wrong kinds of food, nearly drowned him and then lost him.
8. Answers may vary. Yes, Michael loved his pet spider because he tried to be kind to him and was very sad when he thought Webster had been squashed.
9. Answers may vary. No, all animals have certain foods that they should be fed and human food is usually not good for them.
10. Answers may vary. Yes, spiders are good pets to have because they're interesting. OR No, spiders are not good pets to have because they should be left in their own environment.

Unit 2 – Forgetful Friday

1. The character who did not like Fridays was Nelson.
2. Ming was crying because she had lost her glasses.
3. The class had to get off their chairs and try to find Ming's glasses.
4. When the bell went the children got up to go out to recess, but had to stay and do their spelling test instead.
5. Answers may vary. Yes, Miss Fazio was a kind teacher because she asked the whole class to help Ming find her glasses. OR No, Miss Fazio was not a kind teacher because she kept the class in at recess to do the spelling test.
6. No, Nelson obviously did not work hard to remember his spelling words because every test day he forgot them.
7. Yes, Ming was worried about losing her glasses because she was crying.
8. Yes, Nelson often forgets things: he forgets his spelling words, he forgot to look for Ming's glasses and then he forgot to forget his spelling!
9. Answers may vary.
10. Answers may vary. I think Nelson will be good at spelling now because he is more confident and knows he can "forget" to get the words wrong. OR I think Nelson will still be bad at spelling because he has a bad memory and he does not try hard enough.

Unit 3 – Vocabulary 1

2. a) me, put b) tell, part c) through, soup
   d) last, below e) large, around

Unit 4 – Quick Quiz 1

1. a) hungry b) groaned c) Friday d) drowned
   e) catch f) spelling g) plate h) butter
   i) gasp j) recess

Unit 5 – Take Me to Your Leader

1. The name of the alien is Gweep.
2. The alien has a zap gun for a weapon.
3. The alien has tried to take over six planets, including Earth.
4. The alien took back a bowl of lime jelly to his boss.
5. Yes, Tim helped the alien to return to his planet without having to tell his boss that he had failed to take over the Earth.
6. At first Tim was scared but, when he discovered there was only one tiny alien, he thought it was funny and he felt sorry for Gweep.
7. Tim tricked Gweep by saying the jelly was shaking because it was afraid of him.
8. Yes, Gweep was happy because he had the bowl of jelly and could tell his boss that he had taken over the slime on Earth.
9. Answers may vary. Yes, Gweep's journey was successful because he could go home and say he had taken over the slime on Earth and because they named jelly after him. OR No, Gweep's journey was not successful because he failed to take over Earth and had to trick his boss.
10. Answers may vary. When Gweep returned to his planet he was made a hero for taking over Earth and a new jelly was named after him.

Unit 6 – Thing in the Fridge

1. This story begins when the power is turned off and everything in the freezer starts to melt.
2. Blob was born in one of the strange, sticky blobs that began to grow in the slimy lake of food.
3. A trapped fly was the visitor in the freezer.
4. When Thing met the Blob, the cheese growled and rushed at Thing and knocked her over.
5. Thing hid because she was very new and did not know what might happen to her.
6. Yes, the Blob was a bully because he growled at Thing and was violent.
7. Yes, Thing was brave because she stood up to the cheese and defended herself.
8. Thing's life changed living under the fridge because she made friends with the mice, who shared their cheese.
9. Answers may vary. No, bullies usually don't win in the end because nobody wants to be their friend and they end up alone, just like the Blob did.
10. Answers may vary. Yes, it is a good idea to make new friends who you can share and have fun with, because no one likes to be alone all the time.

Unit 7 – Vocabulary 2

1. a) back (1)
   b) of / ten (2)
   c) e / ven (2)
   d) an / oth / er (3)
   e) dif / fer / ent (3)
   f) nev / er (2)
   g) years (1) h) some / thing (2)
   i) to / geth / er (3)
   j) man (1)
2. a) big b) came c) home d) men e) much f) place
   g) saw h) say i) too j) us

ANSWERS

Unit 8 – Quick Quiz 2

2. mistake, freezer, melted, friends, power, scraped, sausages, vegetables, cheese, mice

Unit 9 – Facing Fears

1. Bruno was standing frozen in the playground because a bee was buzzing around him.
2. The one thing Bruno was afraid of was bees.
3. The bee landed on Bruno's nose.
4. Bruno fainted when the bee landed on his nose.
5. Answers may vary. Nelson teased Bruno because he wasn't scared of the bee and he was making fun of Bruno's fear.
6. Answers may vary. Miss Fazio stopped Nelson teasing Bruno because it was making Bruno more frightened and because Nelson was being unkind.
7. Answers may vary. Bruno was afraid that bees would sting him.
8. Miss Fazio suggested that Bruno learn more about bees and why they attack so he wouldn't be afraid of them.
9. Answers may vary. Yes, the more we know about something, and understand why it behaves the way it does, the less fear we should have.
10. Answers may vary. "Facing Fears" is a good title for this story because Bruno comes face to face with a bee, his worst fear, and it is also a message from the author to look at what scares you and try to understand it so it is not so frightening.

Unit 10 – Polar Explorers

1. Explorers have been interested in the polar regions for hundreds of years.
2. The main goals for early Arctic exploration were to chart and navigate the Arctic's coastlines and islands, study the region and be the first to reach the North Pole.
3. Antarctica was first seen by humans in 1820.
4. Many countries sent expeditions to Antarctica to carry out scientific research, claim land, map the continent and compete to be the first to the South Pole.
5. Yes, exploration was hard as the explorers had to battle blizzards, frostbite, hunger, homesickness, exhaustion, cramped living spaces, injury and sickness.
6. Yes, people have lived in the Arctic for thousands of years.
7. Many scientists choose to live and work in the polar regions and the Antarctic is a popular destination for tourists.
8. Explorers risk their lives to explore the polar regions because it is an exciting challenge.
9. Countries wanted to be the first to reach the North and South poles so they could claim the land as their own.
10. People find the North and South poles so interesting because they are so remote and so different from other parts of the world.

Unit 11 – Vocabulary 3

1. a) away b) small c) before d) come e) thought f) any g) left h) asked i) well j) give

Unit 12 – Quick Quiz 3

1. a) I am <u>afraid</u> of the dark.
   b) <u>Bees</u> live in a hive.
   c) Let's meet in the <u>playground</u> after school.
   d) The <u>heart</u> pumps blood around the body.
   e) A <u>fear</u> of heights is called vertigo.
2. a) polar b) mapped c) claimed d) explorers e) dangers

Unit 13 – Technological Wonders

1. The Boeing 747 was introduced in 1970.
2. The Boeing 747 could carry almost three times more passengers than any other aircraft.
3. Even before it was ready for testing, 26 different airlines had ordered Boeing 747s.
4. By 1990, Boeing was producing one new 747 every six days.
5. The freighter version of the 747 has a hinged nose to allow cargo to be loaded through the front of the aircraft.
6. The Airbus A380 is used on popular flights because it is the largest passenger aircraft, so it can carry more people on each flight.
7. The Boeing 747 is still the world's fastest subsonic passenger aircraft.
8. Answers may vary. We want aircraft to fly at such great speed so people can reach their destination as quickly as possible and airlines can offer more frequent flights.
9. Answers may vary. No, the Airbus A380 will probably not remain the largest passenger aircraft forever, because as technology improves so will aircraft.
10. Answers may vary. As the population increases, we will want bigger, faster planes to carry more people on each flight, to get from place to place faster, and so airlines can offer more flights and make more money.

Unit 14 – The Human Body

1. The body has organ systems to keep the everything working and healthy.
2. Cells that are strong can be found in the bones.
3. Cells that send electrical messages can be found in the brain.
4. Groups of cells with a similar function form tissue.
5. If you fall over and scrape your knees, cells can reproduce to replace the damaged tissue.
6. The stomach, liver and small intestine are organs in the digestive system that help us use the food we eat.
7. The brain receives messages about what you see, hear, touch, taste or smell. The brain sends messages to the rest of the body too. It tells the body to do things, such as walk, hop, blink and breathe.
8. The skin is the largest organ of the human body because it covers the body.
9. Answers may vary. No, every living thing begins with one cell that grows and multiplies.
10. Answers may vary. No, we could not live without organ systems, because we need organs to breathe, eat, reproduce, move and think.

Unit 15 – Vocabulary 4

2. Answers may vary. Could include:

```
 n    r    while    b
set   i    e        e
 w    g    n        n
      h    t      still
      take
```

ANSWERS

Unit 16 – Quick Quiz 4

1. a) build b) aircraft c) cruising d) sound e) cargo f) travel g) large h) producing i) speed j) passenger

Unit 17 – Our Future in Space

1. Astronauts eat their food on magnetic trays, with metal knives, forks and spoons.
2. Astronauts sleep in sleeping bags attached to the walls of the station and near a ventilation fan.
3. Astronauts need a ventilation fan to move the carbon dioxide they exhale away so that they can breathe in oxygen.
4. Astronauts need to exercise to keep muscles fit and strong as their legs aren't used much in space.
5. There is only microgravity in a space station, which means very little gravity.
6. Yes, as there is very little gravity, the astronauts would float rather than walk on the floor.
7. Yes, the exercise equipment would need to be attached to the floor or walls of the space station or it would float around.
8. Answers may vary. Yes, astronauts would have to be very fit and strong before entering a space station and have to continue to exercise so they do not lose their muscle tone and mass.
9. Answers may vary. As there are no plants to produce oxygen naturally in the space station, an oxygen supply would have to be provided in tanks to allow the astronauts to breathe.
10. Answers may vary. Yes, without gravity everything would feel very different from how it feels on Earth and the astronauts would have to practise eating, dressing and moving to get used to it and to make sure everything worked properly.

Unit 18 – Life on the Goldfields

1. Life on the goldfields was hard; it was cramped, dirty and often violent.
2. Miners lived in dirty conditions in tents, often with not enough food, poor nutrition and disease.
3. Underground mining work was dangerous because the mines could collapse and bury the miners.
4. Some of the foreign miners were British, American, French, Italian, German, Polish, Hungarian and Chinese.
5. Yes, the monthly fee to mine was 30 shillings, which was about a whole week's wages.
6. No, some miners did not pay their fees and often got into fights with the police.
7. Australia's population doubled and, as Melbourne was the closest port to the goldfields, it soon became Australia's biggest city and financial centre.
8. As towns around the goldfields grew, houses, shops and hotels were built, and theatre, music and sport improved life for the miners.
9. Miners put up with such poor living conditions because they dreamed of finding their fortunes in gold.
10. Answers may vary. Miners who did not find gold would have been very poor and may have had to return to their own countries, or try to find other work in Australia.

Unit 19 – Vocabulary 5

1. Answers may vary.
   a) own, why or old
   b) look or must
   c) between
   d) write, might or going
   e) why, own or old
   f) always
   g) might, write or going
   h) must or look
   i) going, write or might
   j) old, own or why
2. Answers may vary. Here's one possibility:
   Our teachers think because things look like a number they can't be a name but if you looked under the next line you might want the name to be a number.

Unit 20 – Quick Quiz 5

1. a) orbit b) asleep c) float d) sleeping e) station f) astronauts g) Earth h) gravity i) space j) exercising

Test 1 Comprehension

4, 6, 1, 2, 5, 3

Test 2 Comprehension

2, 5, 1, 3, 6, 4

Test 3 High-Frequency Words

Use the numbered high-frequency word cards to check the correct answers.